*How Would Jesus Love?*

CHERYL WHITE

*This devotional is dedicated to my beautiful family and dear friends. Your encouragement and support have been a huge blessing.*

**How Would Jesus Love**
Copyright © 2025 by Cheryl White

Published by Lucid Books in Houston, TX
www.LucidBooks.com

All rights reserved. No part of this publication may be reproduced, stored in a retrieval system, or transmitted in any form by any means, electronic, mechanical, photocopy, recording, or otherwise, without the prior permission of the publisher, except as provided for by USA copyright law.

Unless otherwise indicated, scripture quotations are taken from the (NLT) Holy Bible, New Living Translation, copyright ©1996, 2004, 2015 by Tyndale House Foundation. Used by permission of Tyndale House Publishers, Carol Stream, Illinois 60188. All rights reserved.

Scripture quotations marked (ESV) are taken from the ESV® Bible (The Holy Bible, English Standard Version®), copyright © 2001 by Crossway, a publishing ministry of Good News Publishers. Used by permission. All rights reserved.

Scripture quotations marked (KJV) are taken from the King James Version (KJV): King James Version, public domain.

Scripture quotations marked (NKJV) are taken from the New King James Version®. Copyright © 1982 by Thomas Nelson. Used by permission. All rights reserved.

eISBN: 978-1-63296-783-1
ISBN: 978-1-63296-782-4

Special Sales: Most Lucid Books titles are available in special quantity discounts. Custom imprinting or excerpting can also be done to fit special needs. Contact Lucid Books at Info@LucidBooks.com

# Table of Contents

| | |
|---|---|
| Foreword | vii |
| Introduction | 1 |
| **Part 1:** Daily Devotional | 3 |
| Day 1 | 3 |
| Day 2 | 7 |
| Day 3 | 11 |
| Day 4 | 13 |
| Day 5 | 15 |
| Day 6 | 17 |
| Day 7 | 19 |
| Day 8 | 21 |
| Day 9 | 23 |
| Day 10 | 25 |
| Day 11 | 27 |
| Day 12 | 29 |
| Day 13 | 33 |
| Day 14 | 35 |
| **Part 2:** Christlike Love Put into Action | 37 |
| Conclusion | 51 |
| Special Thanks | 57 |

# Foreword

When asked to write this foreword for *How Would Jesus Love?* I did not have to think twice about what I would write. Cheryl has been my spiritual "Momma" for quite some time.

When I met Cheryl, I was in a very dark place. I was incredibly angry, hurt, and lost. I had not been off the streets and drugs for very long, and I had a lot of guilt and shame, to say the least. We met in church, and then she told me about a group she wanted to start with broken and hurting women. I told her to count me in.

For five years I sat in her living room receiving much ministry and love. I was transformed! Many tears and much healing happened in her house. She is a wonderful woman of God and an amazing counselor.

She is now my pastor, and I have her to thank for where I am today. My self-esteem has grown so much, and I believe in myself, thanks to her.

I work at the local Union Rescue Mission where I have the privilege of praying with and helping broken and hurting people. I am thankful that what I went through prepared me to minister to the precious souls who come through our doors.

I do not think I would be where I am today without Cheryl teaching me to trust in the Lord. She is a wise woman with a heart of gold. She has taught me what love looks like. And I am so happy to call her my friend.

**Angela Harr,**
Executive Secretary
Union Rescue Mission
Fairmont, West Virginia

# Introduction

For years we have heard the saying, "What would Jesus do?" and have seen WWJD on coffee mugs, T-shirts, bracelets, necklaces, and tote bags. It's a solid reminder to us that we should always respond as Jesus would.

Not long ago I was awake in the middle of the night spending some quiet time with the Lord. Suddenly, I heard, "How would Jesus love? I turned to John 15:12 and read, *"Love one another as I have loved you"* (ESV).

Jesus was the perfect example of love. He left the splendor of heaven knowing that He would be crucified on a cross for our sins. What a beautiful display of selfless love: *"For God so loved the world that he gave his only begotten Son, that whosoever believeth in him should not parish, but have everlasting life"* (John 3:16 KJV).

This act of love was a precious gift freely given to us. Jesus laid down His life that we might be reconciled to our heavenly Father. Jesus set the example of what love looks like. As we apply the truths of His teachings to our daily lives, we become more and more like Him.

Jesus said, *"If you love me, you will keep my commandments"* (John 14:15 ESV). His gift to us was salvation. Our gift to Him is obedience.

As you read the pages of this devotional, it is my prayer that you will have a greater understanding of what Christlike love looks like.

I remember the lyrics of a popular 1960s song, which said that all the world needs is love; the songwriter correctly observed that there was too little love in our world. That is certainly the case in the world today where so much hate is promoted instead of love. If we can get a true understanding of what godly love looks like, maybe we can make an impact that would make a huge difference in our troubled world.

Please journey through the pages of this devotional with an open heart and receive all that God has for you.

**How Would Jesus Love (HWJL)?**

# PART 1
# Daily Devotional

# Day 1

*Jesus answered him..."And you shall **love the Lord your God** with all your heart, with all your soul, with all your mind, and with all your strength." This is the first commandment. And the second, like it, is this: "You shall love your neighbor as yourself." There is no other commandment greater than these.*
—Mark 12:30–31 NKJV

*Whoever confesses that Jesus is the Son of God, God abides in him, and he in God. And we have known and believed the love that God has for us. **God is love**, and he who abides in love abides in God, and God in him.*
—1 John 4:15–16 NKJV

Before we can ever begin to love others as Jesus loves, we must first love Him as Mark 12:30–31 states. That takes surrender. True surrender to God comes in an intimate relationship with Jesus Christ. As we give up our desires for His desires, surrender becomes easier. Our attitude should always be, "My whole heart is Yours, Lord, and all my life, I will strive to surrender to you."

*Keep on asking, and you will receive what you ask for. Keep on seeking, and you will find. Keep on knocking, and the door will be opened to you. For everyone who asks, receives. Everyone who seeks, finds. And to everyone who knocks, the door will be opened.*

—Matthew 7:7–8

I encourage you to spend time getting to know Jesus. The New Testament gives great insight into His teachings. We are to follow His instructions. The more we get to know Him by reading the Word, the more we will understand what His love looks like.

## Day 1

Heavenly Father, thank you for sending Jesus Christ to die for my sins. I accept Him as my Lord and Savior. As I seek Him, I will strive to follow Him with my whole heart, soul, mind, and strength. Teach me, through your Word, how to love as Jesus loves. In Jesus's name I pray. Amen.

# Day 2

*I am the true grapevine, and my Father is the gardener. He cuts off every branch of mine that doesn't produce fruit, and he prunes the branches that do bear fruit so they will produce even more. You have already been pruned and purified by the message I have given you.* **Remain in me, and I will remain in you.** *For a branch cannot produce fruit if it is severed from the vine, and you cannot be fruitful unless you remain in me. Yes, I am the vine; you are the branches. Those who remain in me, and I in them, will produce much fruit. For apart from me you can do nothing.*

—John 15:1–5

As I mentioned on day 1, the more we get to know Jesus, the more we will understand what His love looks like. John 15:5 tells us that apart from Jesus, we can do nothing. How can we love others as Jesus does if we are not willing to get to know Him.

> *The sinful nature wants to do evil, which is just the opposite of what the Spirit wants. And the Spirit gives us desires that are the opposite of what the sinful nature desires. These two forces are constantly fighting each other, so you are not free to carry out your good intentions.*
>
> —Galatians 5:17

When we are not feeding our spirit by being in the Word and spending time in prayer with the Lord, we will yield to our flesh (our sinful nature). Jesus told His disciples to *"Watch and pray lest you enter into temptation. The spirit is willing, but the flesh [body] is weak"* (Matthew 26:41 NKJV). It's in feeding our spirit with truth and obeying those truths, that we can learn to "love like Jesus loves." The greatest gift that we can give is love.

## Day 2

Heavenly Father, As I choose to feed my spirit with Your Word, please give me the strength to overcome the temptation to yield to my flesh. In Jesus's name I pray. Amen.

# Day 3

*Love suffers long and is kind; love does not envy; love does not parade itself, is not puffed up; does not behave rudely, does not seek its own, is not provoked, thinks no evil; does not rejoice in iniquity, but rejoices in the truth; bears all things, believes all things, hopes all things, endures all things. **Love never fails**.*

—1 Corinthians 13:4–8 NKJV

These verses are perfect examples of what love looks like. Can we as human beings love in this manner? Yes, we can! Jesus says, *"This is my commandment: Love each other in the same way I have loved you"* (John 15:12).

There are dozens of examples of what Jesus's love looks like throughout the New Testament. Everything is directed back to love. Love God, love one another, and love your enemy. This kind of love can only be accomplished through Jesus Christ. Remember that, in John 15:5, Jesus said, *"Apart from me you can do nothing."*

When we are willing to make Jesus our number one priority, we will surrender our whole life to Him. We will live to please Him and obey Him. His love, which is agape love, is full of grace and mercy; it is unconditional. Jesus Christ showed his agape (selfless, unconditional) love by dying on the cross for the sins of the world. We are to imitate Jesus and walk in love. To do this, we must die to ourselves. *"Those who say they live in God should live their lives as Jesus did"* (1 John 2:6).

> Heavenly Father, help me to love as You love. Search my heart and reveal to me anything that doesn't represent Your love. In Jesus's name I pray. Amen.

# Day 4

*"You have heard the law that says the punishment must match the injury: 'An eye for an eye, and a tooth for a tooth.' But I say, do not resist an evil person! If someone slaps you on the right cheek,* **offer the other cheek also.***"*

—Matthew 5:38–39

How can we turn the other cheek when someone comes against us? It's not easy, but it is required if we are going to love like Jesus loves. Turning the other cheek doesn't necessarily mean that we allow people to do bodily harm to us. Jesus taught that when someone attacks us in a disrespectful way, we are not to defend our rights with revenge or retaliation. The defense of a follower of Christ rests in the hands of our heavenly Father.

*Do all that you can to live in peace with everyone. Dear friends, never take revenge. Leave that to the righteous anger of God. For the Scriptures say, "I will take revenge; I will pay them back," says the Lord.*
—Romans 12:18–19

I often think of the pain and suffering Jesus went through after His arrest. He was beaten and hung on a cross. He was willing to take the blows for our sins. He spoke not a word in retaliation, but He did say, *"Forgive them for they know not what they do"* (Luke 23:34 KJV).

Always remember two wrongs don't make a right. When we "turn the other cheek," we are responding in the same way that Jesus would respond. When we submit to Jesus's teachings, we won't be tempted to respond in an ungodly manner. Search your heart daily and respond as Jesus would.

> Heavenly Father, give me the strength to resist the temptation to retaliate when someone hurts me or attacks my character. Help me to keep my emotions intact and turn the situation over to You. In Jesus's name I pray. Amen.

# Day 5

*"You have heard the law that says, 'Love your neighbor and hate your enemy. But I say, **love your enemies! Pray for those who persecute you!** In that way, you will be acting as true children of your Father in heaven. For he gives his sunlight to both the evil and the good, and he sends rain on the just and the unjust alike. If you love only those who love you, what reward is there for that? Even corrupt tax collectors do that much. If you are kind only to your friends, how are you different from anyone else? Even pagans do that. But you are to be perfect, even as your Father in heaven is perfect."*

—Matthew 5:43–48

It is easy to love and to pray for those who are your friends and family, but it's not so easy to pray for someone who is your enemy. So often, we justify the disdain that we have for those we consider to be our enemies. You certainly can't love them or pray for them in your own strength, but Philippians 4:13 tells me that *"I can do all things through Christ who strengthens me"* (NKJV).

Each of us has experienced betrayal in our lives. Betrayal is very painful. It's heartbreaking when we find out that someone whom we thought was our friend was actually our enemy. But we must respond to our enemies in the way that Jesus would. We must pray for them. I find that when I pray for my enemies, it brings the peace that I need to overcome the pain and the disappointment. It also takes me to a place where I am willing to forgive.

Loving our enemies and praying for them takes us where God wants us to be. As Jesus looked beyond our sins on the cross, we must also look beyond the sins of our enemies.

> Heavenly Father, help me to look beyond the faults of my enemies and give me the desire to love them and pray for them. In Jesus's name I pray. Amen.

# Day 6

*Since God chose you to be the holy people he loves, you must clothe yourselves with tenderhearted mercy, kindness, humility, gentleness, and patience. Make allowance for each other's faults, and **forgive anyone who offends you**. Remember, the Lord forgave you, so you must forgive others.*

—Colossians 3:12–13

Forgiveness is one of the most freeing experiences that you can encounter, and holding onto unforgiveness is one of the most damaging things that you will encounter. Unforgiveness brings anger and bitterness into your soul, and it robs you of your peace and your joy.

> *If you forgive those who sin against you, your heavenly Father will forgive you. But if you refuse to forgive others, your Father will not forgive your sins.*
> —Matthew 6:14–15

Because we are forgiven, we are to forgive others. That is such a simple statement, but forgiving is not always easy to do. So often we feel justified in having unforgiveness in our hearts, but if we are going to love like Jesus loves, we must forgive.

> *I tell you, you can pray for anything, and if you believe that you've received it, it will be yours. But when you are praying, first forgive anyone you are holding a grudge against, so that your Father in heaven will forgive your sins, too.*
> —Mark 11:24–25

Verse 25 tells us that we must forgive and not hold a grudge while we are praying. We have free will, and it's a matter of choice. What will you do?

> Heavenly Father, as You have forgiven me, help me to forgive others. I thank You for the freedom that comes in forgiveness. In Jesus's name I pray. Amen.

## Day 7

*Stand fast therefore in the liberty by which Christ has made us free, and **do not be entangled again with a yoke of bondage**.*

—Galatians 5:1 NKJV

When we hold onto things that are robbing us of the fullness of God, that will drain us spiritually. Jesus came to set us free from the bondage that enslaves us. We can't love others as we should if we are holding onto things that don't line up with what love looks like. Our past hurts can affect our present day.

So often, we justify holding onto our past pain and our anger, and that imprisons us. When we are followers of Christ, we must let go of the past and move forward.

We can never change the past, but through Christ we can change our today and our tomorrows.

> *Therefore, if anyone is in Christ, he is a new creation; old things have passed away; behold, all things have become new.*
> —2 Corinthians 5:17 NKJV

What joy there is in allowing the Lord to remove the pain of your past. Letting go is a choice that you must make if you want to enjoy the freedom that Jesus brings. Luke 4:18 tells us that Jesus came *to* set the captives free.

> *And I will give you a new heart, and I will put a new spirit in you. I will take out your stony, stubborn heart and give you a tender, responsive heart. And I will put my Spirit in you so that you will follow my decrees and be careful to obey my regulations.*
> —Ezekiel 36:26–27

Heavenly Father, give me a new heart that is tender and responsive to You. Help me to realize that I am a new creation in Christ. In Jesus's name I pray. Amen.

# Day 8

*And don't sin by letting anger control you. Don't let the sun go down while you are still angry, for **anger gives a foothold to the devil**.*

—Ephesians 4:26–27

*Understand this, my dear brothers and sisters: You must all be **quick to listen, slow to speak, and slow to get angry**. Human anger does not produce the righteousness God desires.*

—James 1:19–20

There are times when we all struggle with anger. What we do with that anger determines whether we are doing what is right or what is wrong in the eyes of God. Psalm 37:8 says, "Stop being angry! Turn from your rage!

Do not lose your temper—it only leads to harm."

Anger is destructive. It will always lead to ungodly responses. We are to be slow to speak and slow to become angry. The old saying, "count to ten," is a very wise statement. Count to ten or even higher if necessary. Take the wisdom of Proverbs 15:1 to heart: *"A soft answer turns away wrath, but a harsh word stirs up anger"* (NKJV).

When we are angry, we lose control of our emotions. We often say things that we later regret. But once our words are out in the atmosphere, we can't take them back; the damage is done.

> Heavenly Father, help me so that my emotions and my anger will not cause harm. Help me to respond with love as Jesus would. In Jesus's name I pray. Amen.

# Day 9

*The heart of the godly **thinks carefully before speaking**; the mouth of the wicked overflows with evil words.*

—Proverbs 15:28

*The **tongue can bring death or life**; those who love to talk will reap the consequences.*

—Proverbs 18:21

Whoever said, "Sticks and stones may break my bones, but words will never hurt me," was wrong. Our words are powerful. We either speak words that are beneficial or words that are destructive. We must realize that we are accountable for every idle word we speak.

*And I tell you this, you must give an account on judgment day for every idle word you speak. The words you say will either acquit you or condemn you.*
—Matthew 12:36–37

The Bible tells us that we are not to do anything to cause someone to stumble. Our words can do that very thing, so be careful with your words. We are to speak words that build people up, not tear them down. Romans 14:19 says, " *So then, let us aim for harmony in the church and try to build each other up."*

Heavenly Father, help me to control my tongue. Help me to speak words of encouragement, not words that tear down. Help me to be slow to speak instead of speaking out of my emotions. In Jesus's name I pray. Amen.

## Day 10

***Respect everyone,*** *and love the family of believers.*
—1 Peter 2:17a

*Therefore,* ***accept each other*** *just as Christ has accepted you so that God will be given glory.*
—Romans 15:7

There are all kinds of people in the world with different ethnic backgrounds and with different views and opinions. Our differences should not affect our relationships with one another.

If we are to love one another as Jesus loves us, we must love one another through our differences. Unfortunately, we don't see a lot of that in today's society. So many become angry if we don't agree with them. As Christians, we can set the example for others to follow. We may not always be in agreement with one another, but we can agree to disagree and continue walking in love.

Differences of opinion can open doors to conflict. People are going to believe what they believe. If you see that someone's opinion does not line up with God's Word, you can gently share truth with them, but you can't pressure them into conforming to your way of thinking. The best thing you can do is to love them right where they are and remember them in your prayers.

> *Love each other with genuine affection and take delight in honoring each other.*
> —Romans 12:10

Heavenly Father, help me to respond to others as you would. Give me insight in how to respond to our differences. In Jesus's name I pray. Amen.

## Day 11

*For even the Son of Man came not to be served but to **serve others** and to give his life as a ransom for many.*

—Mark 10:45

*For God is not unjust. He will not forget how hard you have worked for Him and how you have shown your love to Him by **caring for other believers**, as you still do.*

—Hebrews 6:10

As Christians, we are all called to serve one another. God has blessed each of us with certain giftings. These giftings are not to be kept for ourselves, but they are to be used to bless others.

*God has given each of you a gift from his great variety of spiritual gifts. Use them well to serve one another.*

—1 Peter 4:10

Have you used your giftings (talents) to bless someone today? Some believers feel that what they have to offer is unimportant or ineffective. That is not so! What you may think is too small to make a difference in someone's life may be the very thing they need.

When a good deed is sown into someone's life, we bring joy to them. In turn, we also experience joy. We reap what we sow. There is such contentment in knowing that you have touched someone with the love of Jesus through your giftings. Your giftings were not given to you for only you. They were given to you so that you can bless others. Make it your daily goal to touch others as God has touched you.

> Heavenly Father, help me to walk confidently in the giftings that You have blessed me with so that I can touch others in the way that I should. In Jesus's name I pray. Amen.

# Day 12

*Jesus replied with a story: "A Jewish man was traveling from Jerusalem down to Jericho, and he was attacked by bandits. They stripped him of his clothes, beat him up, and left him half dead beside the road.*

*"By chance a priest came along. But when he saw the man lying there, he crossed to the other side of the road and passed him by. A Temple assistant walked over and looked at him lying there, but he also passed by on the other side.*

*"Then a despised Samaritan came along, and when he saw the man, he felt compassion for him. Going over to him, the Samaritan soothed his wounds*

*with olive oil and wine and bandaged them. Then he put the man on his own donkey and took him to an inn, where he took care of him. The next day he handed the innkeeper two silver coins, telling him, 'Take care of this man. If his bill runs higher than this, I'll pay you the next time I'm here.'*

*"Now which of these three would you say was a neighbor to the man who was attacked by bandits?" Jesus asked.*

*The man replied,* ***"The one who showed him mercy."***

*Then Jesus said, "Yes, now go and do the same."*
—Luke 10:30–37

***Never let loyalty and kindness leave you!*** *Tie them around your neck as a reminder. Write them deep within your heart.*

—Proverbs 3:3

The story of the good Samaritan is a perfect example of an act of kindness. Are you willing to go the extra mile to help someone? Matthew 25:40b tells us that when we do acts of kindness, we are doing them as unto the Lord: *"I tell you the truth, when you did it to one of the least of these my brothers and sisters, you were doing it to me!"*

> Heavenly Father, help me to have compassion in my heart so that I may do acts of kindness as You would. In Jesus's name I pray. Amen.

## Day 13

*Always be humble and gentle. **Be patient with each other**, making allowance for each other's faults because of your love.*

—Ephesians 4:2

Patience brings peace into our life situations and into our relationships. We are to always strive to be patient.

*Since God chose you to be the holy people he loves, you must clothe yourselves with tenderhearted mercy, kindness, humility, gentleness, and patience. Make allowance for each other's faults and forgive anyone who offends you. Remember, the Lord forgave you, so you must forgive others.*

—Colossians 3:12–13

When things don't happen the way we want them to happen or when people don't act the way we want them to, we can lose our patience. We tend to want what we want, and we want it now! There is purpose in everything we go through.

> *We can rejoice, too, when we run into problems and trials, for we know that they help us develop endurance. And endurance develops strength of character, and character strengthens our confident hope of salvation.*
>
> —Romans 5:3–4

To have patience, we must trust the Lord. He works everything together for our good. His way of thinking and His timing are not like ours. He shows up just at the right time. Psalm 37:3a gives us the key to patience: *"Trust in the Lord and do good"* (KJV).

> Heavenly Father, I choose to put my trust in You and to be patient, knowing that You are working things out on my behalf. In Jesus's name I pray. Amen.

# Day 14

**Let your gentleness be known to all men.** *The Lord is at hand.*

—Philippians 4:5 NKJV

*Pursue righteousness and a godly life, along with faith, love, perseverance, and gentleness.*

—1 Timothy 6:11b

Gentleness is one fruit of the Holy Spirit. We are to display a gentle spirit toward others. To do that, we must choose to walk in humility. A gentle person can bring peace to challenging situations. Each of us should strive to help build healthy relationships and strive to bring good results in conflict. A gentle person displays the character of Christ. When we practice gentleness, we show others what Christlike character looks like. From Proverbs 15:1, we learn that *"a gentle answer deflects anger, but harsh words make tempers flare."*

How easy it is to lose control of our emotions when we are facing tense situations. When we are at a crossroads, we can respond in a way that will escalate the situation, or we can choose to respond as Jesus would. A gentle response can defuse our challenges. It's up to us to make the right decision.

> *And a servant of the Lord must not quarrel but be gentle to all, able to teach, patient, in humility correcting those who are in opposition, if God perhaps will grant them repentance, so that they may know the truth.*
>
> —Timothy 2:24–25 NKJV

Heavenly Father, help me to control my emotions and respond with gentleness as You would. In Jesus's name I pray. Amen.

## PART 2
# Christlike Love Put into Action

Of course, the greatest story of love is the story of Jesus Christ hanging on a cross and dying for our sins. It was the ultimate sacrifice for mankind. But the Bible also includes another great story of love, forgiveness, and reconciliation. That is the story of Joseph (based on selected passages from Genesis 37–46).

Jacob loved Joseph more than any of his other children because Joseph had been born to him in his old age. So, one day Jacob had a special gift made for Joseph—a beautiful robe. Joseph's brothers hated him because their father loved him more than the rest of them. They couldn't say a kind word to him. The story of Joseph's betrayal is told in Genesis 37:5–36:

> *One night Joseph had a dream, and when he told his brothers about it, they hated him more than*

*ever. "Listen to this dream," he said. "We were out in the field, tying up bundles of grain. Suddenly my bundle stood up, and your bundles all gathered around and bowed low before mine!"*

*His brothers responded, "So you think you will be our king, do you? Do you actually think you will reign over us? And they hated him all the more. . . . Soon Joseph had another dream. . . . The sun, moon, and eleven stars bowed low before me! . . . But while his brothers were jealous of Joseph, his father wondered what the dreams meant."*

His brothers were furious! One day Jacob sent Joseph to check on his brothers to see how they were getting along tending their flocks. When Joseph's brothers saw him coming, they began to make plans to kill him.

*"Here comes the dreamer!" they said. "Come on, let's kill him and throw him into one of these cisterns. We can tell our father, 'A wild animal has eaten him.' Then we'll see what becomes of his dreams!" But when Reuben heard of their scheme, he came to Joseph's rescue."* He urged his brothers

not to kill Joseph, but to leave him in a cistern.

*"Reuben was secretly planning to rescue Joseph and return him to his father. So when Joseph arrived, his brothers ripped off the beautiful robe he was wearing.* Then they grabbed him and threw him into the cistern. . . . *Then, just as they were sitting down to eat, they looked up and saw a caravan of camels in the distance coming toward them. It was a group of Ishmaelite traders taking a load of gum, balm, and aromatic resin . . . down to Egypt.*

*Judah said to his brothers, "What will we gain by killing our brother? We'd have to cover up the crime. Instead of hurting him, let's sell him to those Ishmaelite traders. After all, he is our brother— our own flesh and blood!" And his brothers agreed. So when the Ishmaelites, who were Midianite traders, came by, Joseph's brothers pulled him out of the cistern and sold him to them for twenty pieces of silver. And the traders took him to Egypt.*

*Some time later, Reuben returned to get Joseph out of the cistern. When he discovered that Joseph was missing, he tore his clothes in grief. Then he went back to his brothers and lamented, "The boy is gone! What will I do now? Then the brothers killed a young goat and dipped Joseph's robe in its blood. They sent the beautiful robe to their father with this message: "Look at what we found. Doesn't this robe belong to your son?"*

*Their father recognized it immediately. "Yes," he said, "it is my son's robe. A wild animal must have eaten him. Joseph has clearly been torn to pieces!" Then Jacob tore his clothes and dressed himself in burlap. He mourned deeply for his son for a long time. His family all tried to comfort him, but he refused to be comforted. "I will go to my grave mourning for my son," he would say, and then he would weep.*

Joseph's story continues in Genesis 39:1–20:

*When Joseph was taken to Egypt by the Ishmaelite traders, he was purchased by Potiphar, an Egyptian officer. Potiphar was captain of the guard for Pharaoh, the king of Egypt.*

## Christlike Love Put into Action

*The LORD was with Joseph, so he succeeded in everything he did as he served in the home of his Egyptian master. Potiphar noticed this and realized that the LORD was with Joseph, giving him success in everything he did. This pleased Potiphar, so he soon made Joseph his personal attendant. He put him in charge of his entire household and everything he owned. From the day Joseph was put in charge of his master's household and property, the Lord began to bless Potiphar's household for Joseph's sake. All his household affairs ran smoothly, and his crops and livestock flourished. So, Potiphar gave Joseph complete administrative responsibility over everything he owned. With Joseph there, he didn't worry about a thing—except what kind of food to eat!*

*Joseph was a very handsome and well-built young man, and Potiphar's wife soon began to look at him lustfully. "Come and sleep with me," she demanded. But Joseph refused.*

One day Potiphar's wife grabbed Joseph, and when he pulled away from her, she grabbed his cloak and held onto it until her husband came home.

*Then she told him her story. "That Hebrew slave you've brought into our house tried to come in and fool around with me," she said. "But when I screamed, he ran outside, leaving his cloak with me!" Potiphar was furious when he heard his wife's story about how Joseph had treated her. So he took Joseph and threw him into the prison where the king's prisoners were held.*

*The LORD was with Joseph in the prison and showed him his faithful love. And the LORD made Joseph a favorite with the prison warden. Before long, the warden put Joseph in charge of all the other prisoners and over everything that happened in the prison. The LORD was with Joseph and caused everything he did to succeed.*

Pharaoh's chief cupbearer and chief baker were also imprisoned. Both had dreams, and Joseph interpreted them. Joseph said that the cupbearer's dream meant that Pharaoh would reinstate him to his position, but the baker's dream meant that he would be killed. The destinies of the two men happened just as Joseph said they would. Two years later,

Pharaoh had two dreams as described in Genesis 41:8–57:

*The next morning Pharaoh was very disturbed by the dreams, so he called for all the magicians and wise men of Egypt. When Pharaoh told them his dreams, none of them could tell him what the dreams meant.*

The cupbearer remembered Joseph, and Joseph was called upon to interpret Pharaoh's dreams. The dreams foretold that there would be seven years of plenty and seven years of famine in Egypt. Joseph suggested that Pharaoh put someone in charge of all of Egypt and appoint supervisors to collect food during the good years.

*Joseph's suggestions were well received by Pharaoh and his officials. So, Pharaoh asked his officials, "Can we find anyone else like this man so obviously filled with the spirit of God?" Then Pharaoh said to Joseph, "Since God has revealed the meaning of the dreams to you, clearly no one else is as intelligent or wise as you are. You will be in charge of my court, and all my people will take orders from you. Only I, sitting on my throne, will have a rank higher than yours."*

*As predicted, for seven years the land produced bumper crops . . . . Then the seven years of famine began. . . . People from all around came to Egypt to buy grain from Joseph because the famine was severe throughout the world.*

Jacob sent Joseph's brothers to Egypt to buy grain and food. Joseph was governor of all of Egypt and in charge of selling grain to all the people. When his brothers arrived, they bowed before him with their faces to the ground. Joseph recognized his brothers instantly. *"Although Joseph recognized his brothers, they didn't recognize him. And he remembered the dreams he'd had about them many years before"* (Genesis 42:8).

Joseph finally revealed his identity to his brothers when he was alone with them. He broke down and cried. I am sure his brothers were fearful, knowing what they had done to him years before. But Joseph loved them and was thankful that his family was about to be reconciled.

After testing their motivation, he revealed himself to

his brothers (Genesis 45:3, 5):

> *"I am Joseph!" he said to his brothers. "Is my father still alive?" But his brothers were speechless! They were stunned to realize that Joseph was standing there in front of them. . . . Don't be upset, and don't be angry with yourselves for selling me to this place. It was God who sent me here ahead of you to preserve your lives."*

Joseph easily forgave his brothers because he understood that God had sent him to Egypt. Thirteen years passed from the time that Joseph's brothers sold him into slavery to the time he left prison. Even though he was a slave and even though he was imprisoned, God's favor was upon him.

His relationship with his family was restored. He was reunited with his father, his brothers, and their families. What the enemy meant for evil, God turned around for good. And He will do the same for you. God always has your best interest at heart, even when it seems like He doesn't. If you are in the middle of a difficult situation, please remember that God will see you through.

*So be strong and courageous! Do not be afraid and do not panic before them. For the Lord your God will personally go ahead of you. He will neither fail you nor abandon you.*

—Deuteronomy 31:6

Joseph continually moved forward with integrity and trust in the Lord throughout those difficult years. His story should inspire each of us that even though we may face trials, we can come out on the other side of them victoriously.

*I have told you all this so that you may have peace in me. Here on earth, you will have many trials and sorrows. But take heart because I have overcome the world.*

—John 16:33

I pray that you are inspired by Joseph's story. If you are struggling in your love walk, you can be assured that God is with you and that your help comes from Him.

*Yes, I am the vine; you are the branches. Those who remain in me, and I in them, will produce much fruit. For apart from me you can do nothing.*

—John 15:5

We can't change ourselves in our own strength, but we can change through Jesus Christ. We may be weak within ourselves, but He is strong: *"I can do all things through Christ who strengthens me"* (Philippians 4:13 NKJV).

As we go through life, we can develop habits that don't line up to God's Word, but those habits can be broken, and we can find our way to new habits. This doesn't happen overnight. It takes prayer, consistency, and a willingness to please God. First Thessalonians 2:4b reminds us that *"our purpose is to please God, not people. He alone examines the motives of our hearts."*

Is pleasing God your number one goal? It should be, because if it is not, you will never find your way to the wonderful wholeness He can and will bring. It's all about Him, not about you.

> *Dear friends, if we don't feel guilty, we can come to God with bold confidence. And we will receive from him whatever we ask because we obey him and do the things that please him.*
>
> —1 John 3:21–22

It so important to please God. When we do, we can come boldly to Him in confidence, knowing that He will hear our prayers and answer them. He may not always answer our prayers the way we would like, but He will answer them.

> *But seek first the kingdom of God and His righteousness, and all these things shall be added to you.*
>
> —Matthew 6:33 NKJV

Joseph made the best of his very bad situations and continued to trust God. He lived his life striving to please God, and he continually experienced God's favor. Even though Jesus had not come into the world, Joseph knew how to *"love like Jesus would."*

Each of us can also *"love like Jesus loves."* Loving one another as Jesus does is a command, not an option (John 15:12). You can touch the lives of others with God's love simply by obeying His Word. Review the devotional for day 3 to remind yourself of what love looks like (1 Corinthians 13:4–8).

Paul encourages us to walk in the Spirit. We can do that, but it takes discipline and a close relationship with Christ. The closer we walk with Jesus, the more we will love like Jesus. The more we read the Word, the more we will know how to love like Jesus.

Galatians 5:22–23 says, *"But the Holy Spirit produces this kind of fruit in our lives: love, joy, peace, patience, kindness, goodness, faithfulness, gentleness, and self-control. There is no law against these things!"* Is this what people see in you? It's a journey to get to this place, but it is certainly doable through Jesus Christ.

# Conclusion

I would love to tell you that in my everyday life, I have mastered my walk of love, but I can't. I can tell you that I strive to, but there are times when my emotions get in my way. I may not react verbally to people who hurt me or agitate me, but in my heart, I know that my attitude is not matching up to the attitude of Jesus. So, what do I do? I run to the one who can help me, Jesus. The good news is that I run to Him much quicker than I used to.

> *Search me, O God, and know my heart; test me and know my anxious thoughts. Point out anything in me that offends you, and lead me along the path of everlasting life.*
>
> —Psalm 139:23–24

When we allow ourselves to get to the place where we are not justifying our actions or our attitudes, we can find our way to where we need to be: In Jesus! That's why it is so important that we die to our flesh daily. We do that by opening our hearts to the Lord and allowing Him to search us. I can promise you that the Holy Spirit will reveal to you what you need to let go of. It's all about letting go and letting God.

Unforgiveness is the number one sin that will keep us from walking in love and obedience to the Lord. Many years ago, I allowed unforgiveness to nearly destroy me. I was in a very troubled marriage. Through years of being mistreated, I allowed unforgiveness to take me to bitterness, anger, hatred, self-pity, and total defeat. It not only affected me mentally, but it also affected me physically. Oh, but God!

When I finally came to the end of myself and gave all my pain and distress to Jesus, I found the healing that I so desperately needed. Oh, what freedom! If you are harboring unforgiveness in your heart, you can experience the same kind of freedom that I found.

Jesus came to set the captives free. As you are reading these words, there may be some emotions stirring up within you. Our flesh justifies unforgiveness. Several years ago, I wrote a poem that I would like to share with you.

## IT'S NOT AN OPTION

Lord, today someone offended me.
They hurt me with their words.
My carnal nature longs to retaliate.
Their actions were absurd!
My flesh says be angry and unforgiving.
How could they be so cruel?
An eye for an eye, a tooth for a tooth
Should be the golden rule.
I'll hold onto this grudge forever,
and I will be justified in what I do.
After all, they should have held their tongue,
for this there's no excuse!
There's a mighty battle raging inside of me.
My flesh is longing to win,
but my spirit man is rising up,
I must forgive them of their sin.
I know that you can cleanse and set me free
from a response which is so unlike thee.

> Walking in love is not an option,
> but a commandment that you have given me.
> Please renew my mind and change my heart.
> so that I can respond as you would.
> Oh, thank you Lord for the strength you give.
> I long to do as I should.

For years I held onto my pain and unforgiveness. I would pray, "Lord, if you would change my husband, I could be a better Christian." How easy it is to look to others for our happiness and fulfillment in life. Yes, my husband needed to change, but so did I. I finally came to the realization that I was looking to someone instead of looking to the One for my happiness.

Finally, I came to the end of my rope. I needed help! Praise God for my "spiritual mother" who directed me to a way that would rid me of unforgiveness, anger, bitterness, and so much more. No longer could I justify my sin. It was time to surrender, and that is what I did.

Believe me when I say, it was not easy. There was a real battle between my flesh and my spirit. The enemy of my soul wanted me to hold onto all my misery, but God had another plan for me. I found freedom. If you are struggling with unforgiveness, you don't have to stay stuck there. How easy it is to find the speck in someone else's eye when we have a plank (log) in our own.

*And why worry about a speck in your friend's eye when you have a log in your own? How can you think of saying to your friend, "Let me help you get rid of that speck in your eye," when you can't see past the log in your own eye? Hypocrite! First get rid of the log in your own eye; then you will see well enough to deal with the speck in your friend's eye.*

—Matthew 7:3–5

If we would spend more time working on ourselves instead of trying to fix others, we would be much better off. The Holy Spirit doesn't need us to help Him do His job. We are not the "fixer-uppers" of others! We are to be an example for others to follow. We learn in Philippians 2:12 that we are to work out **our own** salvation with fear and trembling.

It is my prayer that this devotional will inspire you to love like Jesus does. Practice makes perfect. Jesus said, *"Love one another as I have loved you."* Love is not an option. It's a commandment. Don't be just a hearer or a reader of the Word. Be a doer of the Word.

The world needs to see what true Christlike love looks like. Will you be the one to show them?

## **HWJL**

*"Love one another as I have loved you."*

—John 15:12

# Special Thanks

Special thanks to my family and friends who have allowed me the privilege of teaching them the HWJL principles.

Also, a special thanks to Gary and Linda Hollingshead for their initial editing before choosing Lucid to publish this devotional. I love all of you.

www.ingramcontent.com/pod-product-compliance
Lightning Source LLC
LaVergne TN
LVHW051528070426
835507LV00023B/3369